D1650380

'Come to this sacred ta

not because you must but because you may;

come, not to declare that you are righteous,

but that you desire to be true disciples of our

Lord Jesus Christ.'

Invitation to Communion

SHARE *this*

feast

reflecting on Holy Communion

For most Christians, since the earliest times, gathering to celebrate Holy Communion has been at the centre of our worshipping lives. Whether held frequently or less often, the service which includes sharing bread and wine is regarded as a feast in which we encounter Jesus Christ present with us now. It is one of the most important ways in which we learn, over time, what it means to be a Christian disciple – and we learn through being nourished and fed.

The Gospel story tells how Jesus shared an intimate Last Supper with his friends before his arrest and crucifixion. He took bread and wine, blessed them, and gave them out, saying 'This is my body' and 'This is my blood,' adding, 'Do this in remembrance of me.' Communion services ever since recall this occasion, when Jesus explained the meaning of his life and death through a meal.

The Church teaches that Holy Communion is a 'sacrament'. It is an act of worship in which we share ordinary material things (bread and wine or grape juice). Through God's grace, the bread, the wine and the gathered people come to embody the transcendent love of God in Christ. When we enter worship, it is 'a time out of time'. Its special and intense focus makes explicit some truths about God, ourselves and the created world, which we are then more fully able to recognize and live out in our daily lives.

Holy Communion has many layers of meaning. This book is based on the nine themes identified in the Methodist Church's report to its Conference of 2003, *His Presence makes the Feast*. However, there is much shared ground between all the Churches that celebrate Holy Communion. There are different practices, and a variety of hymns and prayers are used, but these themes are held in common:

- life in unity
- thanksgiving
- remembering
- sacrifice
- personal devotion
- presence
- the work of the Spirit
- anticipation
- mission and justice.

Using this book

This book will help you reflect and pray about Holy Communion, as it is understood by Christians. The meaning of Communion for you will build up in layers over the course of your life as a disciple, and will be shaped by what you bring of yourself (along with many others) to the 'sacred table' and what you are able, at different times, to receive. For each theme, there is a suggested question for reflection. There are also suggestions on p. 44 for Bible readings to help you explore the theme further.

If you are using this book to prepare to come to Communion, you might wish to focus just on one section each time, and notice how that theme weaves its way through every part of the service.

If you are using it in a group setting, it will again be helpful to take only one theme at a time, and use what is here as a starting point for sharing your experiences and exploring the questions that arise for you. It should be used alongside the usual service book of your Church.

The pattern of the liturgy

Though it can be varied, the service of Holy Communion usually follows a distinctive shape. There are several traditional prayers that are often used, as we:

- gather in God's name
- offer prayers and songs of praise and approach
- confess our sins and receive assurance of God's forgiveness
- hear and respond to readings from scripture, including the Gospel
- pray for the Church and the world
- affirm the faith of the Church
- exchange the Peace
- bring our offerings, including the bread and wine
- pray the Great Prayer of Thanksgiving, including the narrative of the Last Supper
- pray the Lord's Prayer
- break the bread and share Holy Communion
- give thanks and go out into the world with a blessing.

THE NINE THEMES
Contents

'Love bade me welcome … so I did sit and eat.'
George Herbert

Celebrating Holy Communion is always about participating in community. We gather with other Christians, in the name of a God whose very nature is loving community - the Trinity. Communion is not something we can celebrate alone, and, though it always takes place in an actual human community, it isn't a feast that we create. It is something God offers and invites us to. We take our place alongside other people we know, whom we love and maybe struggle with, and in company with all faithful disciples, present and past, who celebrate across the world and before the face of God in heaven. We share together as the 'Body of Christ', the community of his followers.

LIFE IN

*'In the one Spirit
we were all baptized
into one body.
Let us therefore keep
the unity of the Spirit
in the bond of peace.'*
The Peace

The unity that we share in coming to Communion is our unity in Christ. It is not the kind of unity that arises from getting together with 'people like us' – our friends or allies, those who share a similar background, skin colour, gender, or political opinions. As the apostle Paul says, it is not 'your own meal', it is 'the meal of the Lord', and we may find ourselves eating and drinking with a strange bunch of people, whom God has called together.

This famous icon of the Trinity, painted by Andrei Rublev in the 1420s, reflects the Old Testament story where Abraham and Sarah gave hospitality to three heavenly visitors (Genesis 18). The faces are identical and the three convey, through their mutual gaze and body language, a sense of loving community. There is an empty space at the table for those who are looking at the icon, and the Communion cup and food await us.

UNITY

'we are one body'

'Love, like death, has all destroyed,
Rendered all distinctions void;
Names, and sects, and parties fall:
Thou, O Christ, art all in all.'
Charles Wesley

Pray for your own worshipping community.
What signs of 'unity' can you discern there?
How do these differ from those of an ordinary social group?

'Holy and merciful God,
we confess to you,
and to one another,
in communion with all the saints,
that we have sinned through our own fault
in thought, and word, and deed;
in what we have done
and in what we have failed to do.'
Confession

8

'For all who eat and drink without discerning the body, eat and drink judgement against themselves.'

1 Corinthians 11.29

confession

'*There is now no condemnation for those who live in union with Christ Jesus.*'

Assurance of forgiveness

It is significant that in the earliest descriptions we have of Christian communities sharing Holy Communion, we also have evidence of profound social divisions and behaviour that excluded people. In the ancient world where Paul and others were trying to build Christian communities, the idea of social equality between all people was unheard of. Yet Christianity attracted those of many social ranks, from slaves to aristocrats. The church members at Corinth met to worship, but seem to have reproduced their social divisions at the Lord's Supper – even having different things to eat and drink. Paul is critical and demands that Christians should 'discern the body' – the Body of Christ where all are equal.

9

Today, though we come together to celebrate 'life in unity', we are aware of painful, continuing divisions between Christians, divisions which sometimes seem to characterize the Church much more noticeably than its desire for unity. We live in a world where the gulf between rich and poor, within our own society and between different parts of the world, is getting ever wider. Conflict and mutual fear and distrust are all around. When we come to confess our personal sins, we are also acknowledging together our part in all that divides our world, and our Church.

In this image, the Haitian artist Jacques Chéry depicts a mixed world where some people are helping each other, while many are fighting and treading on each other to get to the top of the pile. Above, we see the story of Jesus cleansing the temple, passing judgement on worship that merely reproduces the social and financial exclusions of a divided world.

Another name for Holy Communion is 'Eucharist', which means 'thanksgiving'. At the Last Supper, when Jesus gave thanks and blessed the bread and wine, he was doing something very traditional. He took the elements of a meal and, giving them symbolic significance, linked them to the story of God's dealings with people.

This is why, before we retell the story of the Last Supper, we give thanks for the whole story of 'salvation history'. The Great Prayer of Thanksgiving usually starts with a reference to the Creation story in Genesis, to the Fall (the choice of human beings to disobey God) and to the history of God's people, including the Passover and deliverance from slavery. We praise God for being the kind of God whom we glimpse in this story of salvation – the giver of life and freedom.

THANKS

'he gave thanks'

When we take part in the act of thanksgiving, we are both retelling and effectively putting ourselves inside the story of salvation, of Fall and redemption, as it has been handed down to us. When we describe the Fall, we ourselves own it – 'we rejected your love'. We declare that we are involved. In the same way, we claim our part in redemption. When we compare God's forgiveness with that of the father in the story of the Prodigal Son, it is as if we ourselves are the returning child.

GIVING

In *Africa: Market Day Dreams* Betty LaDuke powerfully conveys the sense that this group of contemplative women are created in God's image. The Holy Spirit in the form of a large bird hovers over them, and we see the same spirit-form reflected in the forehead of each woman.

'Father of all,
we give you thanks and praise,
that when we were still far off
you met us in your Son and brought us home.
Dying and living,
he declared your love, gave us grace, and opened
the gate of glory.'
Post-Communion prayer

'Gladness and pity and passion and pain,
All that is ours and must die –
Lay all before him, return him his gift,
God, to whom all shall go home.'

Peter Icarus

THANKS

12

At the Methodist Conference of 2005, as well as bread and wine, stewards preparing the table laid coloured strips of paper on which all the participants had written down their reasons for confidence in God.

*'It is our duty and our joy,
at all times and in all places
to give you thanks and praise.'*

Great Prayer of Thanksgiving

I n our world and in our personal lives, it often feels difficult to give thanks, especially at times of hardship. But, if we recognize that we stand within a much larger story than just our own place and time, our immediate sufferings are put into a wider perspective.

Just before we pray the Great Prayer of Thanksgiving, we offer to God things that symbolize the harvest of creation (bread and wine), but also the fruits of our own work and effort – most often money – which we are offering for the good of the Church and the world. In doing so we recognize that we are only returning to God what God has given to us for our life and nourishment.

GIVING *our offering*

13

At the same time as laying our gifts on the table, we are also laying open our hearts, the things we struggle with, whatever we have truly brought to worship with us. These will include the specific 'burdens on our heart' that have been expressed in the prayers of intercession for the world. We give our dreams, thanks, fears and struggles to God, so that they may be transformed and used to God's glory.

*'All things come from you,
and of your own have we given you.'*

Offertory prayer

What do you find it easy to be thankful for? What is hard?
How can you make sure you bring all these things to worship?

'Can a woman forget her nursing child, or show
no compassion for the child of her womb?
Even these may forget, yet I will not forget you ...
says the Lord.'

Isaiah 49.15

I n the Bible, living creatures are sustained through being held in the powerful, all-embracing memory of God. For Christians, the greatest evidence that God has not forgotten us is the life, death and resurrection of Jesus Christ. In Holy Communion, we remember God's saving grace in Jesus Christ, and find ourselves named as those whom God has not forgotten.

To 'remember' in the biblical sense is not about idle nostalgia, it is to understand and embody in a present and active way all that we have inherited from those who went before us, and who prepared the ground we stand on. It is to re-enact the story and allow its meaning and power to shape our actions in the present world. In the Old Testament, such 'remembering' is the basis for giving justice to the poor, the vulnerable and the enslaved. The story is to be remembered and retold regularly.

'Remember that you were a slave in Egypt and the Lord your God redeemed you from there; therefore I command you to do this.'

Deuteronomy 24.18

Does the experience of Holy Communion bring
up powerful memories for you? Can you say why
these are important in your walk with God?

'remembrance of me'

*'This is not the table of the Church or the establishment.
This is the table of God and the meal of the Exodus.'*

Andy Braunston

In Harriet Tubman and the Promised Land, Jacob Lawrence envisages Harriet as a young girl during the time of Black people's enslavement in America, hearing the biblical story of the Exodus told by an older woman. Her wide arm gestures communicate the power and energy of the story. As an adult, Harriet herself led an uprising against slavery.

The presiding minister at Holy Communion holds the bread before breaking it and sharing it with the people.

When the Bible speaks of God remembering, it is an active remembering. God does not merely call us to mind, but is present to us in our need. In the same way, when Jesus asks his disciples to remember him, he invites us to be present to him in our need, so that he can meet with us here and now.

When the story of the Last Supper, and the institution of Holy Communion, is retold, we recall that (as with the Passover), the command to remember was given at a time of crisis. It was 'on the night that he was betrayed', and Jesus was sharing a meal not only with friends, but friends who would desert and betray him, who did in fact 'forget', and seek to disclaim their part in his story. To remember is to stay faithful.

'You have commanded us to do
This, in remembrance, Lord of you;
Into our lives your power breaks through,
Living Lord.'

Patrick Appleford

take, eat'

We are asked to remember not only in an
abstract way, but with our bodies. We break
bread, receive, eat, drink and take the elements
into ourselves, so that we cannot disclaim
what these actions declare.

When Jesus commands us to remember him,
he also asks us to act. He asks us to feed the
hungry, to be his hands and feet in the world.
It is the same kind of remembering that is involved in remembering God's commands about
justice – it means enacting them. Reliving the
story strengthens us to keep our promises.
And, as we do as we have been asked, so we
encounter the living Christ.

'As often as we eat this bread and drink this cup
we proclaim the Lord's death until he comes.'

Invitation to Communion

SACRIFICE 'for you'

'Amazing love! How can it be
That thou, my God, shouldst die for me?'
Charles Wesley

At the heart of Holy Communion is the memory of the sacrificial death of Christ. We speak of the bread and wine becoming for us the body and blood of the Lord, and then we eat and drink them. In the ancient world, animal sacrifice was common, and the life of the animal was often offered as a way of atoning for the sins of the community. The practice of Christians made it clear that they believed that the death of Jesus, who was executed as a criminal by the Romans, was the sacrifice to end all sacrifices. By living our human life, and accepting death on a cross, God in Christ has reconciled all things, 'making peace through the blood of his cross' (Colossians 1.20). When we celebrate Holy Communion, we recall this once for all event and seek to share in its meaning and power.

'Jesus, Lamb of God,
have mercy on us.
Jesus, bearer of our sins,
have mercy on us.
Jesus, redeemer
of the world,
grant us peace.'
Agnus Dei (Lamb of God)

Christian artists throughout the ages have tried to open our hearts to the meaning of the cross. As a religious symbol, it is still a shocking one – the image of tortured human being. But the image of the cross is a powerful reminder that faith must be lived in a world where this kind of violence is still only too common. Christians believe that God in Christ has touched the depths of what humans are capable of, and has redeemed and forgiven us even there. There is no suffering that has not been graced by God's presence.

Engelbert Mveng's painting, *Christ in Majesty*, in Cameroon shows Christ surrounded by African martyrs who have given their lives to serve their crucified king. The white, red and black colours of life and death flow through his body and into the robes of his followers. All are a backdrop to the table where Holy Communion is shared here and now.

'With a love stronger than death
he opened wide his arms on the cross.'

Great Prayer of Thanksgiving

Many people have a cross or a picture of the cross that is important to them. If you do, look at it quietly and reflect on what it means to you.

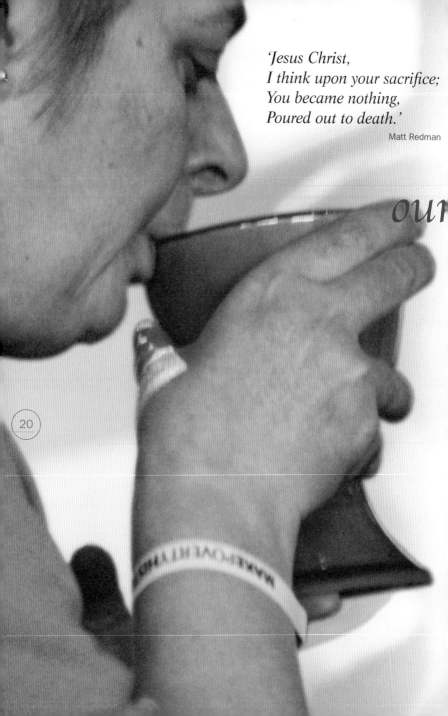

'Jesus Christ,
I think upon your sacrifice;
You became nothing,
Poured out to death.'

Matt Redman

our

*'Through him we offer you our souls and bodies
to be a living sacrifice.
Send us out
in the power of your Spirit
to live and work
to your praise and glory.'*

Post-Communion prayer

SACRIFICE

response

When we were baptized, Paul points out, we were baptized 'into Christ's death', in order that we may also share his risen life. Coming to Holy Communion is a regular reminder to us that we too have made a sacrificial commitment. The Methodist Covenant service reminds us 'I am no longer my own but yours'. We are invited to sacrifice putting ourselves at the centre of our life's meaning, and to surrender to the will and pleasure of God. This is not a special 'new year's resolution' only – it is the promise we make week by week, as we live our ordinary lives.

Not being in control is hard for us: it feels almost unbearable. Yet Christians who have tried to live in this way witness to the freedom and joy this can bring. No one is forced to come to eat and drink, but if we do, we are risking participating in the life and death of Christ. We risk giving up our selfishness and our ego, as this closeness to Christ exposes us to the suffering of the broken world for which Christ died.

'Are you able to drink the cup that I drink?'
Mark 10.38

Each time we drink the cup we consent to share the cup that did not pass Jesus by.

But the sacrifice that is asked of us is not about compulsion or guilt, but about the response of one who knows that they are loved, to the deep and generous love of God.

*'Jesus said: "I am the bread of life.
Those who come to me shall not hunger
and those who believe in me shall never thirst.
Draw near with faith."'*

Invitation to
Communion

PERSONAL

'bread to pilgrim.

*'Our hearts are restless
till they rest in you.'*

St Augustine

Many people feel a sense of awe in approaching Holy Communion, and a corresponding sense of being unworthy to be present and to receive the elements. Several of the Communion prayers acknowledge this. We 'do not presume' to approach the table 'trusting in our own righteousness'. We declare 'Lord, I am not worthy to receive you'. Yet we do in fact approach, ask for the word of healing, claim the crumbs from the Lord's table.

And it is right that we should not hold back. It is true that we are never, through our own goodness, going to 'earn' what is offered here. The bread of life is offered to us where we are, as nourishment for the journey, as satisfaction for our deep hunger for what is most real – a hunger that nothing else but God alone can satisfy.

Peter initially resisted having his feet washed by his Lord. Many who have low self-esteem, or who have been bullied or abused, find it desperately hard to know and accept the respect that Christ offers them, as an honoured guest. All of us are astounded by the humility of our Saviour, who lovingly challenges our refusal to let ourselves receive – and meets us there.

given'

The Indian artist Jyoti Sahi's painting *Washing the Feet* recalls the story in John's Gospel of Jesus washing Peter's feet at the Last Supper. It is confusing at first glance, because it is natural to see the figure on the right as Jesus, using a gesture of blessing. But in fact Jesus is the figure on the left, almost bent double, in the posture of a lowly servant.

*'We strain to glimpse your mercy-seat,
And find you kneeling at our feet.'*
Brian Wren

'I come with joy to meet my Lord,
Forgiven, loved, and free,
In awe and wonder to recall
His life laid down for me.'

Brian Wren

Throughout the Gospels, Jesus is shown sharing meals with a whole variety of people. In the ancient world, to share food with someone, whether as the host or the guest, was an important gesture of intimacy, which was thought to create a powerful bond of mutual loyalty. Scandalously, Jesus is seen sharing hospitality with a wide range of people: his closest friends, his religious opponents, corrupt tax collectors and several disreputable women. It is during mealtime conversations (sometimes heated) that much of his teaching is given. And one of his classic images of the kingdom of God is a feast – a feast where the respectable are invited, but to which they send their apologies as they have prioritized other things. In the end, the feast is attended by those who never expected to be on anyone's guest-list – the poor, the street-dwellers, those without the distractions of wealth and choice.

We are invited to the feast, and asked to hold out our hands and receive the bread of life. It is part of our Christian discipleship, regularly to acknowledge our need and put ourselves in the position to receive this 'means of grace' along with our fellow Christians, and so grow in our love and devotion to our Lord.

How easy or hard do you find it to hold out your hands for what God offers?

DEVOTION
out our hands

'Thank you for bringing us …
where the empty are filled,
and the filled are emptied;
where the poor find riches,
and the rich recognize their poverty;
where all who kneel and hold out their hands
are unstintingly fed.'

Kate Compston

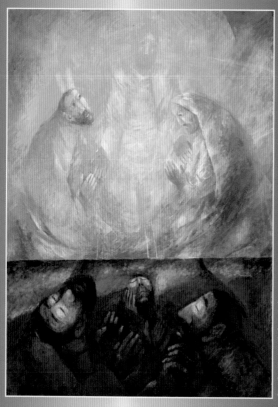

Sieger Köder's painting *Wonder* depicts the story of Jesus' Transfiguration (Mark 9.2-8). On a mountain top, Jesus' closest disciples witness a revelation of Jesus in glory, accompanied by Moses and Elijah. It is as if a veil is lifted from ordinary life allowing his glory to be seen.

PRESENCE
'his presence

'His presence makes the feast;
And now our spirits feel
The glory not to be expressed,
The joy unspeakable.'

Charles Wesley

Within the veil I now would come,
Into the holy place,
To look upon thy face.'
Ruth Dryden

Christians across the ages have fought each other and been willing to die to defend particular teachings about the meaning of the 'real presence' of Christ in the sacrament of Holy Communion. Churches and individual Christians today still differ about how it should be explained, or represented in worship through particular gestures or practices.

But we share an understanding that we are speaking of a mystery, and of an encounter with the risen Christ that is more than a simple memorial of his death. In the Gospels, Jesus promises that 'where two or three are gathered in my name, I am there among them' (Matthew 18.20), and the celebration of Holy Communion is a special example of how this promise is fulfilled. Christ is encountered, not simply in the bread and wine, but in the gathering of the community of believers and in the sharing of bread and wine, as we have been told to do.

nakes the feast'

The story of Jesus' Transfiguration may provide a helpful image of what is happening at Holy Communion. It is a time when we have been invited to draw apart so that our eyes may be opened to underlying truths about God's presence and glory. God is always with us, but we do not always notice and acknowledge this. Holy Communion can offer us a glimpse of this reality.

'For now we see in a mirror, dimly, but then we will see face to face. Now I know only in part; then will I know fully, even as I have been fully known.'

1 Corinthians 13.12

In the Old Testament, there are several stories in which people have dreams, visions, or awesome revelations of the presence of God. To those who have this experience, it seems remarkable that they have survived – 'I have seen God face to face, and yet my life is preserved' (Genesis 32.30). By comparison with Jacob's struggle with an angel in the night, Isaiah's great vision in the temple, or Elijah's 'still small voice' following the earthquake, wind and fire, simply receiving bread and wine at Holy Communion may seem tame.

And yet, anyone who has been privileged to distribute the elements at Holy Communion has seen the open and vulnerable faces of those who receive. It is not unknown for people to weep. This is normal. Not everyone will feel

PRESENCE

Holy Communion

moved in the same way, but all come with a desire to know God and to allow themselves to be truly known. John Wesley understood Holy Communion to be itself a 'converting ordinance'. There is a way in which the invitation to Communion is a renewed call for commitment. Christ died for each, and Christ died for all – this is why it is never appropriate to judge those who receive bread and wine alongside us.

Peter and the others wanted to cling to the Transfiguration experience, but they had to go back down the mountain. Similarly, we cannot cling to the moment of Holy Communion.

'As we gaze on your kingly brightness
So our faces display your likeness,
Ever changing from glory to glory:
Mirrored here, may our lives tell your story.'

Graham Kendrick

THE WORK

'Cleanse the thoughts
of our hearts
by the inspiration of
your Holy Spirit,
that we may perfectly
love you ...'
Prayer of approach

I n Mark's Gospel, when Jesus, Peter, James
and John come down from the mountain
of the Transfiguration, they come across
the rest of the disciples who have been trying,
and failing, to heal a boy who is possessed by
a spirit that sends him into convulsions. The
striking painting by John Reilly, *The healing of
the lunatic boy* (above), depicts the scene where
Jesus himself heals the child. In the dark and
tormenting image on the right, the boy is thrown
to the ground, fearful and struggling, while his
anxious and angry parents (or perhaps they are
disciples) also flail around helplessly. But on
the left of the picture, Jesus stands upright and
immensely calm, his hands offering a blessing.
With his eyes on Jesus, the boy also stands
up, full of strength and dignity. Both figures are
bathed in the light of the Spirit of God.

Your Spirit gives light,
  but we have preferred darkness;
your Spirit gives wisdom,
  but we have been foolish;
your Spirit gives power,
  but we have trusted in our own strength.'
Confession

F THE SPIRIT
pour out your Spirit'

There is a point in the Holy Communion service when we call upon the Holy Spirit. But there is a real sense in which it is the Holy Spirit who has already prompted us to get up and come to worship; who has helped us to pray when we cannot find words; who has stilled our troubled and distracted hearts. Rowan Williams describes us as being like a 'wriggly child' who resists letting an adult do up their coat buttons. The Spirit says 'stand still and let me get at you!'

The story of the boy's healing reminds us that not all spirits are good – we can be gripped by forces that are destructive. We need intentionally to put ourselves in the way of receiving God's Spirit.

Have you been aware of the Holy Spirit working in your life or in the world around you? How do you know it is God's Spirit?

THE WORK (

I n the Holy Communion service, when we ask for the Spirit to be poured out on the gifts of bread and wine, we also ask that we ourselves may be transformed and refashioned in the image of God. This is part of the meaning of being in the presence of Christ, which, when recognized, is always a converting experience. There is a call to repentance and forgiveness, a call to become more truly who we are meant to be, in the presence of God. The Bible uses many images of the powerful Spirit of God: breath, wind, fire. The Spirit searches our heart, comforts and holds us, turns our lives upside down, helps us to pray when we can't find the words, gives us wisdom and integrity, and sends us out with power.

Many different styles of worship may enable us to open up and to put ourselves at the disposal of God's Spirit. For some, quietness and focus are important. Others need joyful music that resonates with our bodies and emotions and releases us from our over-controlling and anxious minds. But in all, the marks of the Spirit are never limited to a particular kind of worship experience, or to a temporary sense of trans-cendence. They are about how the Spirit 'works' on us to bring about transformation in our lives, and show forth real and Christlike 'fruit': love, joy, peace, patience, kindness, generosity, faithfulness, gentleness and self control.

F THE SPIRIT

transformation

'*Spirit of the living God,*
fall afresh on me.'

Daniel Iverson

'*Generous and holy God,*
pour out your Spirit
that these gifts of bread and wine
may be for us the body and blood of Christ.
Refashion us in your image
that we may be found ready
at the coming of our Lord Jesus Christ.'

Invocation of the Holy Spirit

ANTICIPATIO

'a foretaste of

'Your kingdom come.
Your will be done,
on earth as it is in heaven.
Give us this day our bread for tomorrow.'
Matthew 6.10-11 (variant reading)

In the Gospels, there are two versions of the distinctive prayer that Jesus taught his disciples, and what we know as the Lord's Prayer is a combined text. But scholars are agreed that the prayer which perhaps feels quite gentle and comforting to us (because we know it so well) is about the passionately longed for 'end-time'. The reign of God will prevail on earth, and the poor will be liberated from debt, hunger and the grip of violence. We are not only asking for the 'daily bread' which keeps us going, but to be given today 'our bread for tomorrow'. We are urgently praying for a token of that great feast which God has promised to us all.

'*Heaven shall not wait*
For triumphant Hallelujahs,
When earth has passed and we reach another shore:
Jesus is Lord
In our present imperfection;
His power and love are for now and then for evermore.'
John Bell

N
the heavenly banquet'

Christians believe that Holy Communion is a 'foretaste of the heavenly banquet prepared for all people'. This is true of the bread and wine that we share, but the theme of 'anticipation' is indicated at other points in the service also. For instance, the exchange of the Peace symbolizes the full, joyful communion of the life of heaven. In a broken and divided world (and perhaps between people who currently find each other irritating or difficult), the handshake or embrace we give each other declares that God will bring true reconciliation and peace such as the world does not yet know. We do not yet have full communion with each other, but in Holy Communion we name our longing for it, and participate in the longing of our Lord.

'Dying you destroyed our death,
rising you restored our life:
Lord Jesus, come in glory.'

Great Prayer of Thanksgiving

ANTICIPATI

'as a little child

We may be familiar with sentimental Victorian images of gentle Jesus among the children, but when he first offered teaching which used a child as the model for a disciple, it was probably a shock. Children share with other excluded groups, such as foreigners, poor people and people with illnesses or disabilities, the experience of being disregarded, overlooked and not taken seriously. Jesus drew such people to him and taught us that the very authority and status which adults value (and which children or 'little ones' lack) are a block to entering the kingdom.

No-one, perhaps, but a little child is so open about experiencing the excitement of 'anticipation'. By watching them, adults can begin to rediscover their own fresh sense of longing, trust, and expectation of joy.

Make a list of all the things you long for. Then try and look at the list with the eyes of God. What does God long for, for you and your community?

In fulfilling Christ's command to 'remember', the past and present are brought together as we declare our involvement in the story of salvation. In the same way, through 'anticipation', we declare our hope in God's future and our commitment to act as if that future were already present in our midst.

Children commonly also receive the bread and wine; this reflects the promised company of the Kingdom, where all are equal and all are included in the feast.

'Let the little children come to me; do not stop them; for it is to such as these that the kingdom of God belongs. Truly I tell you, whoever does not receive the kingdom of God as a little child will never enter it.'
Mark 10.14-15

'Go forth and tell! The doors are open wide:
Share God's good gifts - let no one be denied.'
J. E. Seddon

The whole movement of the worship at Holy Communion is towards being sent out to share this feast. The nourishment that we receive is not for ourselves alone, but in order that God may empower us to go out into the world, find out what God is doing there, and join in. The experience of worship reminds us that we are created to love God and enjoy God for ever. But there is a sense in which our earthly worship can never be whole, while the world remains fractured. If we have been caught up in the love of God, then we will also long, with God, for the healing of the world.

So the end of the service is only the beginning of what we are asked to do next. Orthodox Christians speak about 'the liturgy beyond the liturgy', which is doing the work of God in caring for the world and bringing knowledge of God's saving love in Christ to all.

John's story of the feeding of the 5,000 has encouraged Christians throughout the ages to recognize that what we have to offer, small though it may be, can be taken and used to unexpected effect through God's grace. We have prayed for each other and for the world during our worship – now we translate these prayers into action.

MISSION &
'to live and work to G

Ethiopian artist Alemayehu Bizuneh depicts the scene in John's Gospel (John 6.1-14) where Jesus miraculously feeds 5,000 people who have come out into the desert to hear him teach. A small boy offers five loaves and two fishes, and Jesus is able to take this gift and transform it.

'To fill each human house with love,
It is the sacrament of care;
The work that Christ began to do
We humbly pledge ourselves to share.'
Fred Kaan

When you are at worship, be attentive to what may be God's word for you. What is the 'sacrament of care' to which you may be called?

JUSTICE

od's praise and glory'

I n recent decades, churchgoers have been active beyond the bounds of their church buildings, and have taken to the streets with many others to protest against war and to campaign for fair trade on behalf of the world's poor. In this political activity, they have put themselves within an honourable tradition of fighting for justice on the basis of Christian faith and biblical values. In the same way, Christians of the past campaigned for the emancipation of enslaved people, for an end to child labour and for working people's rights, and for rights for women, especially the most marginalized. Christians have also founded schools, hospitals, hospices and children's homes. They have established community centres and places where people of many faiths and none can come together to learn from each other and build trust.

'May we who share Christ's body live his risen life;
We who drink his cup bring life to others;
We whom the Spirit lights give light to the world.
Keep us firm in the hope that you have set before us,
So we and all your children shall be free,
And the whole earth live to praise your name.'
Post-Communion prayer

JUSTICE
of care'

We do not 'earn' the grace of God through our actions. But if we do not act on the grace that we have received, our faith is meaningless. The Bible is very tough on those who say 'Lord, Lord', but do not do God's will in the world, on those who are content to feast while others starve, and on those who offer regular and devoted worship but do not actively love our neighbours as ourselves.

We worship a God whose very nature is to hear and respond to the cry of the needy, and we are asked to be the hands and feet of such a God in today's world.

'The trumpets sound, the angels sing,
The feast is ready to begin.'

Graham Kendrick

Sieger Köder
- *The Supper*

Be still,
  look,
  for someone is
  reaching out,
  breaking bread,
  pouring out wine,
  sharing a meal
  with his friends.

Be still,
  listen,
  for someone is
  speaking,
  a voice breaking
  into the darkness
  of the world:
  'My body,
  my blood;
  do this in
  remembrance of me.'

Be still,
  touch,
  for the Lord is here,
  present among us,
  broken for you,
  poured out for many,
  waiting to transform our lives.

INVITAT

Be still,
     taste,
          for here is living
          bread,
          living water,
          the answer to our
          deepest hunger,
          the end of our
          search for truth.

Be still,
     listen,
          for someone is
          calling,
          a voice breaking
          into your darkness,
          speaking your name.

Come now,
     and feed
          in your hearts with
          thanksgiving.

Come now,
     and be filled to
          overflowing.

Nick Fawcett

ON
to the feast

Bible passages for

LIFE IN UNITY

Genesis 18.1-15 (Abraham and Sarah entertain angels unawares); *1 Corinthians 11.23 – 12.31* (The first description of the Lord's Supper, and a discussion about the Church as the Body of Christ).

THANKSGIVING

Genesis 1-3 (Two versions of the story of Creation and Fall); *Luke 15.11-32* (The story of the Prodigal Son).

REMEMBERING

Deuteronomy 6; 24.10-22 (The Israelites are told to remember their deliverance from slavery); *Isaiah 49.14-23* (A prophecy that God will not forget); *Mark 14* (Jesus' disciples betray and desert him).

SACRIFICE

Mark 10.17-45; 12.28–44 (The meaning and cost of discipleship); *Romans 6.1-11* (United in Christ's death and resurrection); *1 Corinthians 1.18-31* (The folly of the Cross); *Philippians 2.1-11* (God's self-emptying love); *Hebrews 4.14 – 5.10* (The sacrifice to end all sacrifices).

PERSONAL DEVOTION

Matthew 11.28-30 ('I will give you rest'); *Luke 14.1-24* (The story of the Great Feast); *John 6* (Jesus - the Bread of Life); *John 13.1-20* (Jesus washes his disciples' feet).

further reading

PRESENCE

Genesis 32.22-32 (Jacob wrestles with an angel); **1 Kings 19** (Elijah's vision of God on Mount Horeb); **Isaiah 6** (Isaiah's vision of God in the Temple); **Mark 9.1-13** (Jesus' Transfiguration); **Luke 24.13-35** (Walk to Emmaus - Jesus is known in the breaking of bread); **1 Corinthians 13** (Love knows us fully); **2 Corinthians 3.4 – 4.18** ('The veil is removed').

THE WORK OF THE SPIRIT

Ezekiel 37.7-14 (The valley of the dry bones); **Mark 9.14-29** (The healing of the epileptic boy); **Acts 2.1-21** (The day of Pentecost); **Galatians 5.16-25** (Fruit of the Spirit).

ANTICIPATION

Matthew 6.5-15 (The Lord's Prayer); **Matthew 11.25-27** (Truth revealed to children); **Mark 10.13-16** (People brought children to Jesus); **Luke 11.1-13** (The Lord's Prayer).

MISSION AND JUSTICE

Isaiah 1.12-17 (Worship without justice offends God); **Matthew 5.1-16** (The Beatitudes); **Matthew 25.31-46** (The story of the sheep and the goats); **Luke 16.19-31** (The rich man and Lazarus); **John 6.1-14** (The feeding of the crowd); **James 2.1-7; 14-17** (Faith without works is dead).

Resources

Bible – a good modern translation such as the New Revised Standard Version (NRSV), the Revised English Bible (REB), the New Century Version or the New International Version (NIV).

Methodist Worship Book, Common Worship, Worship: from the United Reformed Church or the usual service book of your worshipping community.

Hymns & Psalms – The hymnbook of the Methodist Church. It has been said that Methodists 'sing their theology'. Many of the hymns of Charles Wesley contain profound reflections about Holy Communion.

A modern hymnbook such as *Mission Praise, Songs of Fellowship, Let's Praise, Common Ground.*

The Methodist Prayer Handbook - published annually (available September).

His Presence Makes the Feast – report to the Methodist Conference 2003 on the range of ways Methodists understand and practice Holy Communion.

The United Reformed Church Prayer Handbook – published annually (available November). Contact bookshop@urc.org.uk.

Children and Holy Communion, Diana Murrie and Steve Pearce, published by Kevin Mayhew 2003. Includes Church of England background, six session course and copiable 'take home' sheets.

My Communion Cube and **My Communion Book,** Diana Murrie and Craig Cameron, published by Church House Publishing. Contains clear language and absorbing illustrations, to help children understand Holy Communion. Available from mph.

Called by Name – similar in size and style to *Share this Feast,* exploring what it means to be a member of the Methodist Church

The Methodist website - www.methodist.org. uk Methodist Church House (including the Methodist Bookshop) 25 Marylebone Road, London, NW1 5JR Tel: 020 7486 5502

Methodist Publishing House (mph) 4 John Wesley Road, Werrington, Peterborough PE4 6ZP Tel: 01733 325002 Fax: 01733 384180 www.mph.org.uk E-mail: sales@mph.org.uk

Acknowledgements

The material in this book has been prepared by Janet Morley and Jane Leach on behalf of the Methodist Church, in consultation with the Faith and Order Committee of the Methodist Church and many other readers.

1 - Invitation to Communion, *Methodist Worship Book (MWB)*, p. 158.

6 - From 'Love', George Herbert.
- The Peace, *MWB*, p. 177.

7 - *Hymns & Psalms (H&P)* 764, v. 5, Charles Wesley.

8 - Confession, *MWB*, p. 145.

9 - 1 Corinthians 11.29, *New Revised Standard Version of the Bible (NRSV)*.
- Assurance of forgiveness, *MWB*, p. 175.

10 - Great Prayer of Thanksgiving, *MWB*, p. 124.

11 - Post-Communion Prayer, *MWB*, p. 140.

12 - H&P 623, v. 3, Peter Icarus © used with permission of McCrimmon Publishing Co Ltd, Great Wakering, Essex SS3 0EQ

13 - Great Prayer of Thanksgiving, *Common Worship: Services and Prayers from the Church of England (CW)*, p. 184.
- Offertory prayer, *CW*, p. 291.

14 - Isaiah 49.15, *NRSV*.
- Deuteronomy 24.18, *NRSV*.

15 - © Andy Braunston, from *Courage to Love*, compiled by Geoffrey Duncan (London, DLT, 2002)

17 - 'Lord Jesus Christ' by Patrick Appleford (H&P 619, v. 2), © 1960 Josef Weinberger Limited. Reproduced by permission of the copyright owners.

- Invitation to Communion, *MWB*, p. 217.

18 - *H&P* 764, v. 1, Charles Wesley.
- Colossians 1.20, *NRSV*.
- *Agnus Dei*, *MWB*, p. 219.

19 - Great Prayer of Thanksgiving, *CW*, p. 201.

20 - Extract taken from the song 'Jesus Christ I think upon Your Sacrifice' by Matt Redman. © 1986 Thankyou Music. Adm. by worshiptogether.com songs excl. UK & Europe, adm. by kingswaysongs. com tym@kingsway.co.uk. Used by permission.

21 - Post-Communion Prayer, *CW*, p. 182.
- Covenant Prayer, *MWB*, p. 288.
- Mark 10.38, *NRSV*.

22 - Invitation to Communion, *MWB*, p. 196.
- Prayer of humble access, *MWB*, p. 195.

23 - *H&P* 500, v. 3, Brian Wren. Reproduced by permission of Stainer & Bell Ltd.

24 - *H&P* 610, v. 1, Brian Wren. Reproduced by permission of Stainer & Bell Ltd.

25 - © Kate Compston from *Bread of Tomorrow*, edited by Janet Morley (London, SPCK/Christian Aid, 2004)

26 - *H&P* 614, v. 3, Charles Wesley.

27 - Extract taken from the song 'Within the Veil' by Ruth Dryden. © 1978 Genesis Music/ kingswaysongs.com

tym@kingsway. co.uk for Europe & Commonwealth (excl. Australia & New Zealand). Used by permission.
- Matthew 18.20, *NRSV*.

28 - 1 Corinthians 13.12, *NRSV*.
- Genesis 32.30, *NRSV*

29 - From verse 3 of 'Shine Jesus Shine', Graham Kendrick, © 1987 Make Way Music. www. grahamkendrick.co.uk.

30 - Prayer of approach, *MWB*, p. 185.

31 - Confession, *MWB*, p. 174.

32 - H&P 777, Bessie Porter Head.
- Galatians 5.22, *NRSV*.

33 - Invocation of the Holy Spirit, *MWB*, p. 126.
- Daniel Iverson, 'Spirit of the living God', © 1963 Birdwing Music/ EMI Christian Music Publishing Inc. adm. by Kevin Mayhew Ltd and reproduced by permission, licence nr. 604082/3.

34 - Matthew 6.10-11, (variant reading), *NRSV*.

35 - 'Heaven shall not wait', v. 5. Words: John L Bell & Graham Maule © 1987 WGRG, Iona Community, Glasgow G2 3DH. Used by permission.
- Post-Communion prayer, *MWB*, p. 197.

36 - Great Prayer of Thanksgiving, *CW*, p. 192.

37 - Mark 10.14-15, *NRSV*.

38 - H&P 770, v. 5, Words: James Edward Seddon. © The representatives of the late James Edward Seddon/Jubilate Hymns. Used by permission.

39 - H&P 619, v. 3, Fred Kaan. Reproduced by permission of Stainer & Bell Ltd.

40 - Post-Communion prayer, *MWB*, p. 140.

41 - From verse 1 of 'The Feast', Graham Kendrick. © 1989 Make Way Music. www.grahamkendrick.co.uk.

42 - Invitation, Nick Fawcett. Reproduced from *Prayers for all seasons Book 2* by permission of Kevin Mayhew Ltd, Buxhall, Stowmarket IP14 3BW (www.kevinmayhewltd.com), licence nr. 603082.

Quotations from *The New Revised Standard Version of the Bible* (Anglicized Edition) © 1989, 1985, Division of Christian Education of the National Council of the Churches of Christ in the United States of America. Used by permission. All rights reserved.

Quotations from *The Methodist Worship Book* (Peterborough, mph, 1999) © Trustees for Methodist Church Purposes (TMCP). Used by permission.

Quotations from *Common Worship: Services and Prayers for the Church of England* (London, Church House Publishing, 2000) © The Archbishops' Council 2000. Reproduced by permission.

IMAGES

Cover: The Risen Christ by He Qi (www.heqiarts.com). Used with permission.

6 *The Holy Trinity*, 1420s (tempera on panel) by Rublev, Andrei (c.1370-1430), Tretyakov Gallery, Moscow, Russia/The Bridgeman Art Library. Used by permission.

8 Image No. 7 *Without Orientation* and image no. 8 *More than a Temple* from the Misereor Hunger Cloth from Haiti, by Jacques Chéry, © MVG Medienproduktion, Aachen, Germany, 1982.

11 Betty LaDuke, *Africa: Market Day Dreams*, Ashland, Oregon, USA. Author: *Africa through the eyes of woman artists* (Trenton, New Jersey, Africa World Press, 1991). Used by permission of the artist.

15 Reprinted with the permission of Simon & Schuster Books for Young Readers. An imprint of Simon & Schuster Children's Publishing Division from *Harriet Tubman and the Promised Land* by Jacob Lawrence. Copyright © 1968, 1993 Jacob Lawrence.

19 *Christ in Majesty*, fresco on the apse of the Chapel Libermann College in Douala, Cameroun, by Engelbert Mveng. Permission sought from Fr Mveng's estate.

23 *Washing the Feet* by Jyoti Sahi. Used with permission.

26 © Sieger Köder, *Verklärung (Wonder)*. Used with permission.

30 *The healing of the lunatic boy*, by John Reilly from the Methodist Church Collection of Modern Christian Art. © Trustees for Methodist Church Purposes, used by permission of the Trustees of the Collection.

34 *Embrace of Peace II*, by George Tooker.

39 Image no. X from the Misereor Hunger Cloth from Ethiopia, by Alemayehu Bizuneh, © MVG Medienproduktion, Aachen, Germany, 1978.

42 Image no. 3 *The Supper* from the Misereor Hunger Cloth *Hope for the Marginalised*, by Sieger Köder, © MVG Medienproduktion, Aachen, Germany, 1996.

PHOTOS

3 © Guzelan Ltd

4 © Philip Wolmuth

12, 16, 18, 20, 25, 37 © Jane Leach

33 © Mark Zaccaria

41 © Christian Aid

ISBN: 1-85852-322-2
EAN: 978-1-85852-322-4